FAITH, HOPE, LOVE,
and a Whisk

Faith, Hope, Love, and a Whisk

Breakfast with the Savior

Tori Winkelman

Ambassador International

GREENVILLE, SOUTH CAROLINA & BELFAST, NORTHERN IRELAND

www.ambassador-international.com

Faith, Hope, Love, and a Whisk

Breakfast with the Savior

ISBN: 978-1-62020-273-9
eISBN: 978-1-62020-375-0

Photography by Hannah Nichols, Greenville SC

Design & Page Layout by Hannah Nichols
Ebook Conversion by Anna Riebe
Author Photo by Carolyn Abacherli

AMBASSADOR INTERNATIONAL
Emerald House
427 Wade Hampton Blvd.
Greenville, SC 29609, USA
www.ambassador-international.com

AMBASSADOR BOOKS
The Mount
2 Woodstock Link
Belfast, BT6 8DD, Northern Ireland, UK
www.ambassador-international.com

The colophon is a trademark of Ambassador

Printed in China

DEDICATION

I dedicate this book to the Lord. My only desire is to serve Him to the best of my ability, and I can only pray that this book will bring glory to His Kingdom. I also dedicate it to my loving husband, Aaron, who has been my strength, my supporter, and such a godly leader. Also to my wonderful Dad and Mom, who gave me the ultimate gift of teaching me who Jesus, my Savior is, who raised me to put God first, and who taught me to always rely on Him. Finally, my last dedication goes to my beautiful sister, Tawni, who has an amazing heart for Christ and who has been there for me through thick and thin.

My voice You shall hear in the morning, O Lord; In the morning I will direct it to You, and I will look up.

~ Psalm 5:3

FOREWORD

I have had the pleasure of knowing Tori since she was the little child who grew up into the attractive and talented young married woman she is today. I've seen her grow in her skills and style. It is very rare in today's cultural climate to see and know a woman who wants to serve other women with faith, food, and devotion to our Lord with style.

What you see, read and cook from these pages are who Tori is. She truly has a passion for the homemaker to be a godly reflection in all areas of their life. I am pleased to introduce and endorse Tori into your kitchen and home. In one beautiful production, she will guide you into creating for your family and friends what it is like to love your God through each recipe and devotional thought. This beautiful book is truly a breakfast with the Savior.

-Emilie Barnes, speaker,
author of *More Hours in My Day*

Tori and Aaron

Mom and Dad

Grandma and Grandpa Dunkle

Grandma and Grandpa Fachner

INTRODUCTION

To me, the kitchen is the heart of the home. Some of my fondest childhood memories come from sitting around the kitchen table with my family. Each day, after sitting down at the table, my dad would bless the food, and then we would talk, laugh, and tell stories about our day while enjoying the beautiful meal my mom had prepared. It was something so simple; but it drew our family closer together. When my husband and I got married, we knew we wanted our future family to have the same type of closeness to each other and to God.

Faith, Hope, Love, and a Whisk: Breakfast with the Savior combines my two passions in life: God's Word and cooking. It is designed to bring you closer to the Lord and to bring your family around the kitchen table. It is a different type of devotional, one you can read while you are making breakfast or brunch for your family and friends. In John 21:12, Jesus said to His disciples to "Come and eat breakfast," and this cookbook devotional invites you to do the same, in both a literal and figurative way. The devotionals I have written are for women who want to develop a deeper relationship with Jesus and live their life for Him. Everything we do, we do for the Lord—even cooking! So start your morning with Jesus. When you open up this cookbook to find a breakfast recipe, read the devotional while you're cooking, and spend time in prayer with the Savior.

CONTENTS

A Living Example

Be devoted to one another in love. Honor one another above yourselves. Never be lacking in zeal, but keep your spiritual fervor, serving the Lord. Be joyful in hope, patient in affliction, faithful in prayer. Share with the Lord's people who are in need. Practice hospitality.

~ Romans 12:10–13

These verses in Romans are a beautiful example of Christian living! This world we live in is not our home, we are only passing through, but while we are here we need to be living a life worthy of the calling of Christ. We can break these verses up into two categories: how we are to treat others and how we should conduct ourselves. These two things not only define the type of person we are, but how we define ourselves as a representative of Christ.

Courtesy and kindness seem to be a lost art these days, but the Bible tells us to behave differently. As our verse says, we are to be devoted in love, to honor one another, provide for those in need and to be hospitable to one another. When we are living for Jesus, we should hunger to serve others whether they are a friend, a coworker, the homeless or even someone in your family. Jesus says in Matthew 22:39, "And *the* second *is* like it: You shall love your neighbor as yourself." It is so easy to snub that person who is always rude to you or to overlook the sadness in someone's eyes, but even something as small as a smile can make a difference. These seem like such simple acts, but when put into practice they can touch people's lives in a profound way that only Christ can.

How we conduct ourselves as Christians is just as important as how we treat others.

We are told to be joyful in hope, but what does this mean? Our hope is in Jesus Christ, and this verse is saying that we should be joyful in Christ in all aspects of our lives. We should have joy in the good and bad areas of our life because we know that our hope is found in Jesus Christ—He is in control of all things. That is something to be excited about! In his introduction in 1 Timothy 1:1, the apostle Paul even declares Jesus as his hope: "Paul, an apostle of Jesus Christ, by the commandment of God our Savior and the Lord Jesus Christ, our hope."

Being patient in affliction is a little bit harder to do. When we suffer afflictions, it seems as if our whole life is upside down and it is so hard to patiently wait for the affliction to be over. That's where prayer comes in. If we are faithfully praying and calling on the Lord, especially in a time of suffering, the Lord will be faithful to us and will hear our cries. Patience will come with relying on Jesus and having a continual spiritual thirst to be near Him.

These illustrations of how to be a living example for Jesus should be written on our hearts and minds. Not always are they easy to do, especially when trials come our way, but the blessings that come with obeying God's Word are unfathomable! You never know who is watching you, and how God is working on someone else's heart through your words and actions.

Two Pigs in a Blanket

This recipe is dedicated to my husband, who is a big fan of this delectable dish.

How do you make pigs in a blanket even better, you ask? You add bacon!

Ingredients:

2 cups Flour

4 tablespoons Sugar

2 teaspoons Baking Powder

1 teaspoon Baking Soda

Dash of Salt

2 cups Buttermilk

2 teaspoons Vanilla

2 Eggs

6 tablespoons Butter, Melted

⅛ cup Water

½ pound Maple Bacon

12-ounce package Maple Sausage Links

In a large skillet, cook the bacon until crisp; set aside to cool. Note: You can also crisp the bacon in the microwave by putting a paper towel over a microwavable plate, placing the bacon in a single layer over the paper towel, putting another paper towel over the layer of bacon, and microwaving anywhere between 5 and 7 minutes.

In a large bowl, combine the first 5 ingredients. Whisk in the vanilla, buttermilk, and egg until smooth. Then add the melted butter and the water. With your hands, crush the crisp bacon over the batter and stir until combined.

On a large skillet over medium-high heat or on a griddle that's heated to 325 degrees, use a ladle to spoon the batter onto the griddle. Cook until pancake is golden brown; then flip. This will make around 14 to 16 pancakes, depending on how large you make them. While the pancakes are cooking, cook the sausages as instructed on the package.

To prepare the two pigs in a blanket, place one sausage in the middle of the warm pancake, wrap it and secure with a toothpick. Serve with butter and homemade maple syrup. (See page 143 for recipe)

Shadrach, Meshach and Abednego replied to him, "King Nebuchadnezzar, we do not need to defend ourselves before you in this matter. If we are thrown into the blazing furnace, the God we serve is able to deliver us from it, and he will deliver us from Your Majesty's hand. But even if he does not, we want you to know, Your Majesty, that we will not serve your gods or worship the image of gold you have set up."

~ Daniel 3:16–18

These three young men, Shadrach, Meshach, and Abednego can teach us a lot about trust, faith, and devotion through their trials. To stand up to the king of their time and tell him that they will not submit to worshipping a false god takes a lot of faith. Even more faith when they know they are going to be thrown into a fiery furnace to their death.

They were given the choice, and it could have been so easy for them to submit to the worldly law that King Nebuchadnezzar commanded, but they chose God's law instead. Their response to the king was that God is able. If they are thrown into the blazing fire, God is able to save them if it is His will, but if it is not, then they are willing to give up their lives for Him.

We are going to face many trials in our life where Satan is going to try to turn up the heat, but we have a choice of how we handle our trials. We can choose to stay and face those trials with the faith that God will deliver us, or we can succumb to them, too afraid to face the fire. Satan wants us to fold under the pressure and give in to the heat, but we need to stand strong in our faith; don't let Satan win!

When gold is put into fire, it is easy to mold, it is made brighter and shinier, and when it's finished the goldsmith can see his reflection in it. Think of the goldsmith as God and ourselves as the gold. He allows us to endure these trials to refine us, to make us more like Him, and to allow us to shine brighter for His Kingdom.

If you continue to read Daniel 3, you will see that Shadrach, Meshach, and Abednego were thrown into the fire but were delivered by God without a single burn. Are you willing to put your faith in God to get you through the trial you may be facing today? If you are faithful to Him in the tough times of your life, He will never abandon you. He will stay right by your side when the fire seems to be the hottest.

BAKED FRENCH TOAST

This is not only a recipe, it's a tradition. Waking up on Christmas morning to the delicious smell of warm butter and sweet caramelized pecan French toast are some of my fondest memories. Hopefully this recipe will give your family years of tradition and sweet memories too.

INGREDIENTS:

2 loaves of French Bread, cut into 2-inch slices

3 cups Milk

8 Eggs

1 teaspoon Cinnamon

1 teaspoon Nutmeg

1 teaspoon Vanilla

1 stick Butter (softened, use on bread)

TOPPING:

1 stick Butter (softened)

1 cup Brown Sugar

2 tablespoons Dark Corn Syrup

¾ cups Chopped Pecans

Heavily butter the bottom and sides of a 9 x 13 Pyrex dish. Lightly butter both sides of the bread slices and place as many as you can inside the dish, squishing them together to fit.

In a small bowl, whisk together milk, eggs, cinnamon, nutmeg, and vanilla. Pour mixture over the top of bread, making sure to cover every slice with the mixture. Cover with foil and let sit in the fridge overnight—this is mandatory.

In the morning, preheat the oven to 350 degrees and make the topping as follows:

Mix all ingredients together in a small bowl and spread over the top of bread. Put it into the oven and bake for 45 minutes or until medium brown. (Note: If you don't like pecans or if you have a nut allergy, just omit them. It tastes just as good without them.)

GOD FIRST

I urge, then, first of all, that petitions, prayers, intercession and thanksgiving be made for all people—for kings and all those in authority, that we may live peaceful and quiet lives in all godliness and holiness. This is good, and pleases God our Savior.

~ 1 Timothy 2:1–3

I went to Azusa Pacific University, a Christian college where "God First" was the school's motto. This slogan stuck with me even after I graduated. I believe that putting God first is the most important thing we, as Christians, can do. How we do this is through prayer. Bringing everything to God first strengthens our relationship with our spouse, family, children, church, friends, and coworkers.

Whether we are asking for forgiveness, seeking guidance, or giving thanks to the Lord, our prayers should be directed to Jesus on a daily basis. Prayer is pleasing to God. These verses tell us not only to pray for our family, but also for our country, the ones who govern over us, for the believers and the non-believers. As a woman, wife, or mother, this is so important for us to do in order to preserve a God-centered household. Dinnertime is not the only time we should put aside for prayer. Urge your family to bring everything before Jesus first. Anytime I ask my parents for advice, even to this day, the first thing that they say to me is, "Have you prayed about it?" Keep that question on your heart as a reminder to go to God first.

Praying helps keeps our life going in the right direction. If our prayer life is suffering, how do we know if our life is on track? We need Jesus to guide us through this dark world we live in. His path is always the right one. When we pray, it is important to ask for Jesus's will to be done, not ours. Sometimes we get off His path and start to stumble, but when we pray He picks us up and leads us in the right direction. Are you going to God first? Do you know if you are living in God's will? If you don't, take this time to ask Jesus to help you and your family get back to being centered around Him.

MEXICAN STRADA CUPS

This is a Mexican fiesta in a cup. This is my go-to breakfast recipe because you just throw everything together and bake it up; it's as simple as that.

INGREDIENTS:

8 large Eggs

1 can Creamed Corn

2 seven-ounce cans of Diced Green Chiles, drained

1½ cups Milk

3½ cups Sharp Cheddar Cheese, shredded

1 tablespoon Worcestershire Sauce

Sour Cream, Tabasco, and Salsa for serving

Preheat the oven to 350 degrees.

In a large bowl, whisk together the eggs, creamed corn, green chiles, milk, 2½ cups cheddar cheese, and Worcestershire sauce. Take your cupcake tin and coat it well with cooking spray. Then, using either a ladle or a spoon, pour the mixture into each cup, filling it almost to the top; sprinkle the extra cheddar cheese on the top of each cup.

Bake for 45 minutes or until the tops are lightly browned, then let cool for 10 minutes. With a knife, trace the sides on each cup to prevent from sticking and scoop them out with a spoon. Don't worry if there is liquid at the bottom of the tin: it is just juice from the green chiles. Makes 24 servings. Serve with salsa, sour cream, and Tabasco.

(Note: This can also be made in a 9" x 13" Pyrex dish.)

Through the Lord's mercies we are not consumed, because His compassions fail not. They are new every morning; great is Your faithfulness. "The Lord is my portion," says my soul, "therefore I hope in Him!"

~ Lamentations 3:22–24

TO BE OR NOT TO BE . . . A DOER OF THE WORD

Do not merely listen to the word, and so deceive yourselves. Do what it says. Anyone who listens to the word but does not do what it says is like someone who looks at his face in a mirror and, after looking at himself, goes away and immediately forgets what he looks like. But whoever looks intently into the perfect law that gives freedom, and continues in it—not forgetting what they have heard, but doing it—they will be blessed in what they do.

~James 1:22–25

If you have ever heard someone use the term "lukewarm Christian," these verses are what defines that phrase. A lukewarm Christian is someone who claims to be a follower of Jesus but does not show it in their actions. We want to show the world that Christians are different, that we don't say one thing but live another. Our words and actions need to match up. How can you be a witness to your friends or family if being a Christian has no difference on your lifestyle? Ask yourself if you are going to be a woman of the Word or a woman of the world?

James says that saying but not doing is like looking in the mirror and, after going away, forgetting what your face looks like. Think of the mirror as the Bible, the Word of God, and the image of Christ is what we should be reflecting in our lives. If we just read the Bible but forget to do what it says, our witness to others will fail and we won't reap the blessing that God promises us in verse 25.

So how do we go from being just hearers of the Word to being doers of the Word? By changing the way we think. Make it a point, when you go to church, to apply the pastor's sermon to your life that week. Or when you're reading your daily devotions, try to pick out a verse that you can memorize. These are just a few examples of how to condition your mind to focus in the right direction. If God's Word is constantly on your mind, then His image will start to shine out through your actions.

NOTES:

LEMON BLUEBERRY BREAD PUDDING

Bread pudding for breakfast, you say? Yes, please! I can't stop my mouth from watering when I think about this amazing bread pudding! If you are a big bread pudding fan, you will fall in love with this recipe.

INGREDIENTS:

½ loaf French Bread, cut into one-inch cubes

12 ounces Fresh Blueberries

1 quart Whole Milk

3 Eggs, beaten

2 cups Sugar

1½ tablespoons Vanilla

3 tablespoons Lemon Juice

¼ teaspoon Nutmeg

1 teaspoon Cinnamon

3 tablespoons Unsalted Butter, melted

SAUCE:

½ cup Butter

1 cup Cream (Not heavy cream)

1 cup Sugar

1 Egg Yolk

1 teaspoon Vanilla

½ tablespoon Lemon Zest

1 tablespoon Lemon Juice

1 tablespoon Flour

Preheat the oven to 350 degrees.

Butter a 9" x 13" Pyrex dish and layer the bread pieces and blueberries with the last layer being the blueberries. Pour entire quart of whole milk evenly over the bread and set aside.

In a small bowl, mix together the eggs, sugar, vanilla, lemon juice, nutmeg, cinnamon, and melted butter. Pour over the bread and blueberries making sure you hit every visible bread cube on the top.

Cover with foil and bake for 55 minutes to an hour, or until lightly brown.

SAUCE:

While the bread pudding is cooking, whisk all ingredients in a saucepan over medium-to-low heat, stirring rapidly and making sure the egg doesn't divide into little chunks. As soon as the bread pudding comes out of the oven, immediately pour the sauce over the top. Let sit for 10 to 15 minutes before serving.

_____
_____
_____
_____
_____
_____
_____
_____
_____
_____
_____
_____
_____
_____
_____
_____
_____
_____
_____
_____
_____

STRENGTH THROUGH WEAKNESS

I am worn out from my groaning. All night long I flood my bed with weeping and drench my couch with tears. My eyes grow weak with sorrow; they fail because of all my foes. Away from me, all you who do evil, for the Lord has heard my weeping. The Lord has heard my cry for mercy; the Lord accepts my prayer.

~ Psalm 6:6–9

Have you ever felt so worn out at the end of the day that you put your head on the pillow and cry? You are physically and mentally exhausted. Your heart is so weighed down with worries about the bills, your children, the housecleaning, and being a loving wife, all at the same time. The Lord knows our exhaustion; He knows all the pain that we go through. In Mark 4, when Jesus fasted for forty days and forty nights, He was exhausted. Not only was He overcome with exhaustion, but on top of that the devil was trying to tempt Him in various ways.

When we feel completely overwhelmed by the burdens of our life, that is when satan will take the opportunity to try and prey on our weaknesses. 1 Peter 5:8 says, "Be alert and of sober mind. Your enemy the devil prowls around like a roaring lion looking for someone to devour." In order to fight against this, we need to seek the Lord in prayer. He will hear us when we call upon His name. In our verse, David says, "away from me, all you who do evil, for the Lord has heard my weeping." There is not one tear that goes unseen in God's eyes. He sees your struggles—all you have to do is seek Him for help and He will come to your rescue.

God wants us to rely fully on Him because only He can carry our burdens. Jesus lived a perfect and blameless life; not once did He give in to any of the Devil's temptation. I want to challenge you today to fully rely on Jesus when those burdens get too heavy. Just remember 2 Corinthians 12:9: "But he said to me, "My grace is sufficient for you, for my power is made perfect in weakness. Therefore I will boast all the more gladly about my weaknesses, so that Christ's power may rest on me." Give it all to Jesus because when we are weak, He is strong.

GREEN ONION, EGGS, AND HAM QUICHE

This quiche has simple ingredients that pack a punch.

INGREDIENTS:

16 ounces White Mushrooms, washed and sliced

2 tablespoons Extra Virgin Olive Oil

⅓ cup chopped Green Onions

2 tablespoons Butter

8 Eggs

1½ cups Heavy Cream

2½ cups grated Swiss Cheese

1 teaspoon Black Pepper

1 teaspoon Salt

8 ounces Ham, diced

1 Premade Pie Crust, pressed into a 9-inch deep-dish pie pan (If you'd rather make this from scratch, see page 133 for Savory Crust Recipe)

Preheat the oven to 400 degrees.

In a medium skillet over medium heat, sauté the mushrooms in the olive oil for about 8 minutes or until golden brown. Add the green onions and butter, and sauté for another 5 minutes. Set aside.

In a large bowl, whisk together the eggs and the heavy cream. Stir in the Swiss cheese, salt, pepper, the mushroom mixture, and diced ham. Pour the mixture into the prepared pie shell. Loosely cover with foil (make sure you spray the foil with cooking spray so it doesn't stick to the top) and bake the quiche, covered, for 45 minutes.

Then uncover and bake for another 10 minutes. Let cool for about 20 minutes and serve.

SEASONED WITH SALT

Be wise in the way you act toward outsiders; make the most of every opportunity. Let your conversation be always full of grace, seasoned with salt, so that you may know how to answer everyone.
~ Colossians 4:5–6

Food that is seasoned with salt tastes better—it brings out the juiciness in a steak and it gives flavor to those bland pasta noodles. Jesus gives us that salt and flavor in our lives when we have a personal relationship with Him. The "outsiders" in verse five are the nonbelievers of this world. As Christians, our actions are always being watched; the world is always watching to see if we will fail. That is why we need to pray for wisdom so that when we have encounters with nonbelievers they can see the difference in our lives. Being a witness through our actions and words can impact people without us even knowing it. That is what being a genuine follower of Christ is all about: having the image of Christ shine through us.

In every conversation we have, it should be our goal to have that salt that Jesus gives to us show through our words. In Matthew 5:13, Jesus says, "You are the salt of the earth. But if the salt loses its saltiness, how can it be made salty again? It is no longer good for anything, except to be thrown out and trampled underfoot." Christians who don't reflect Christ's words or actions are like salt without saltiness. They aren't good for anything because they aren't striving to further the kingdom of God or even further their own relationship with God, for that matter. The difference between believers and nonbelievers is in the salt.

We should always be looking for opportunities to season other people's lives with the grace of God, in hopes that they might come to know the Lord. So this is my question to you: Are you being the salt of the earth, trying to further the Kingdom of God? Are your words and actions different from the world's? If they aren't, ask the Lord to show you the areas in your life that might be holding you back from being salt for Him.

Always ask God to bless you with opportunities to share the salt and light that you have in your heart. When these opportunities come your way, you will have a blessed conversation that is abounding in grace and seasoned with salt.

CANDIED BACON

This is one of my mom's specialties; she makes it as a side dish for breakfast at Easter.

INGREDIENTS:

1 Pound of Thick Bacon

½ cup Brown Sugar

1 tablespoon Dijon Mustard

Place the brown sugar and mustard in a 1-gallon bag. Knead the bag until all the ingredients are combined. Add one bacon piece at a time, making sure you coat each piece of bacon well with the mixture.

Place bacon strips on a wire rack that has been set on top of a baking sheet. Bake in the oven on 400 degrees for 25 minutes or until crisp (depending on the thickness of your bacon).

SATISFY US IN THE MORNING WITH
YOUR UNFAILING LOVE, THAT WE
MAY SING FOR JOY AND BE GLAD
ALL OUR DAYS.

~ PSALM 90:14 NIV

THIS IS MY OFFERING

A tithe of everything from the land, whether grain from the soil
or fruit from the trees, belongs to the Lord; it is holy to the Lord.
~ Leviticus 27:30

The Lord has given us so much. He gives us a roof over our heads, food to eat, clothes to warm us, and the ultimate gift of salvation and eternal life. What are we giving back to Him? Yes, we sacrifice one hour out of our Sunday morning each week, but is that really enough for our Creator who drops everything to listen intently to our daily prayers, who carries us through the storms of our lives, and who equips us with everything we need for each day? We can never give back to God the amount that He has given to us, but we can offer a portion of what we have.

There are many ways we can serve the Lord. One main act of worship is through tithing a portion of our paycheck back to the church. Not only is this supporting the administrators in our church, it is giving back to God just a slice of what He has graciously blessed us with. In Genesis 28:20–22, we see this act of worship demonstrated, "Then Jacob made a vow, saying, "If God will be with me and will watch over me on this journey I am taking and will give me food to eat and clothes to wear so that I return safely to my father's household, then the Lord will be my God and this stone that I have set up as a pillar will be God's house, and of all that you give me I will give you a tenth.""

Another offering you can give the Lord is the act of service: taking time out of your day to volunteer in the church, with the children's services, or volunteering outside of the church in your community. Matthew 25:35–36 says, "For I was hungry and you gave me something to eat, I was thirsty and you gave me something to drink, I was a stranger and you invited me in, I needed clothes and you clothed me, I was sick and you looked after me, I was in prison and you came to visit me."

Spending more time in God's Word, reading the Bible each day, is also another act of worship. Developing a deeper relationship with Jesus and growing in Him will open up more doors and different ways in which you can serve Him. Ephesians 4:11–12, "So Christ himself gave the apostles, the prophets, the evangelists, the pastors and teachers, to equip his people for works of service, so that the body of Christ may be built up." In whatever way we choose to worship the Lord we need to do it with a cheerful heart. He is fully committed to us, therefore we need to be fully committed to Him. What will your offering be this day?

NOTES:

SWEET POTATO HASH BROWNS

These hash browns have a pretty hue and are a fun alternative to regular hash browns.

INGREDIENTS:

2 large Sweet Potatoes, peeled

4 tablespoons Canola Oil

1 teaspoon Pepper

1 teaspoon Salt

Preheat the oven to Broil.

Using a food processor with a cheese grater attachment or the large holes of a box grater, shred the potatoes. Heat the canola oil in a large 12-inch skillet over high heat. Once hot, pour in the shredded potatoes, pepper, and salt. Using a spatula, start to fold the potatoes inwards until they start to soften: usually about 10 minutes. When they begin to brown, take them off the heat.

Transfer the potatoes onto a greased cookie sheet and spread them into a thin half-inch layer. Put them in the oven and broil them for about 5 minutes. It you want the top to be crispier then you can broil them longer, but watch to be sure they don't burn. Serve with butter.

Makes about 4 servings.

EYES OF THE HEART

Your eye is the lamp of your body. When your eyes are healthy, your whole body also is full of light. But when they are unhealthy, your body also is full of darkness. See to it, then, that the light within you is not darkness.

~ Luke 11:34–35

We live in a world that revolves around entertainment. Movies, musicals, plays, music concerts, sporting events, and so much are all around us. However, not everything is good for our minds, because what we watch, listen to, and partake in will affect our daily lives. That is why we need to train our minds in the ways of the Lord so that we can have eyes that see what is pleasing to Him. If our hearts reflect the image of Christ, then we can be a light to those who are living in the dark.

Proverbs 27:19 says, "As water reflects the face, so one's life reflects the heart." Take a look at your own life right now. What music are you listening to in the car? What shows do you have recorded on TV? What is your main source of entertainment when you go out with your friends? If your answer to any of these questions raises uncertainty in your heart about whether or not they are okay to do, then just ask yourself one last question: Would I do this with Jesus Christ sitting right next to me? If the answer is no, then your lifestyle needs to change.

What we choose to put into our minds will eventually come out in our actions. If we choose to entertain our minds with all of the sin of this world, we become numb to seeing what God's righteousness is. Satan tries to trick us into thinking that everyone does it, everyone watches it, and that it's okay if we do, too. If we start to believe the lies of Satan, we begin to make them truths in our heart, letting darkness overpower the light.

So how can we battle against the tricks that Satan tries to fool us with? We need to listen to the Holy Spirit when He speaks. If you feel like it may be a bad idea to watch that R-rated movie that just came out or listen to that song by the controversial artist, then that is the Holy Spirit prompting your heart to stop and turn away from it. He wants our eyes, ears, and hearts to be healthy so that we can pierce through any darkness that Satan may try to throw our way. Can others see the light that the Holy Spirit has ignited in your heart? Make sure that your eyes are focused on Jesus and that your hearts are reflecting His light.

PINEAPPLE BRUNCH PUNCH

The name says it all. I love serving this at brunches, tea parties, special occasions, you name it, and

it's a huge hit with kids!

INGREDIENTS:

48 ounces canned Crushed Pineapple

48 ounces canned Pineapple Juice

6 Bananas, mashed

1 can Frozen Concentrated Orange Juice (16 fluid ounces)

1 can Frozen Concentrated Lemonade (12 fluid ounces)

3 cups Sugar

10 cups Water

6 Ziplock Bags, 1 gallon each

6 1-liter bottles of Sprite

In a large pot or bowl, mix together the first seven ingredients. Fill 3 bags half-way, seal out all the air, and close. Double all the bags and freeze upright in the freezer overnight. An hour before your brunch or event, take out one of the gallon bags, place in a punch bowl, and with a spoon, chop at it to break it into large chunks. Pour in a whole liter of Sprite, stir, and enjoy! Once the punch gets low, take out another bag, chop it up, and add another liter of Sprite. Serves about 12 people.

THE VIRTUOUS WOMAN

She is clothed with strength and dignity; she can laugh at the days to come. She speaks with wisdom, and faithful instruction is on her tongue. She watches over the affairs of her household and does not eat the bread of idleness. Her children arise and call her blessed; her husband also, and he praises her: "Many women do noble things, but you surpass them all." Charm is deceptive, and beauty is fleeting; but a woman who fears the Lord is to be praised.

~ Proverbs 31:25–30

These verses are so crucial to a Christian woman's life, and something that each of us should strive after on a daily basis. I would have loved to write out all of chapter 31, so I encourage you to read it when you get a chance. What is a virtuous woman? Webster's dictionary describes the word virtuous as "morally excellent." Our world today mistakes beauty for virtue, physical fitness for strength, and successful careers for not partaking in the bread of idleness. While all of these things are perfectly fine to have, they are not what make up a virtuous woman. A virtuous woman, at the core, has a heart for God. So, let's break down each of these verses so we can see what virtues God expects us to have.

The first two verses are all about our demeanor and our words. In verse 25, we are to clothe ourselves each day with respect for ourselves and others, strengthened by our relationship with Jesus. In verse 26, notice how it says, "wisdom and faithful instruction is on her tongue"; it means that she has not yet spoken it. Women (including me), can often be too quick to speak without thinking. Listen to your husband, children, family, boyfriend, and friends first, and then speak with the wisdom that God gives you after prayerfully considering your words. Not out of anger or foolishness, but with wisdom and faithfulness. James 1:19–20 tells us, "My dear brothers and sisters, take note of this: Everyone should be quick to listen, slow to speak and slow to become angry, because human anger does not produce the righteousness that God desires."

Verses 27 through 29 are all about how we are to act within the comforts of our home. A virtuous woman takes care of her household, not only in regard to cleaning, but also in keeping an orderly home. It is our responsibility to watch over the affairs of our children because the Lord has given them to us as a blessing. We need to be their guiding light, showing them the ways of the Lord, which is why it is important for us to be actively involved in their lives. Proverbs 22:6 says, "Start children off on the way they should go, and even when they are old they will not turn from it." An orderly, godly household will not only bring you and your husband closer together, but the whole family will be blessed by the Lord. Psalms 112:1–2 says, "Praise the Lord. Blessed are those who fear the Lord, who find great delight in His commands. Their children will be mighty in the land; the generation of the upright will be blessed."

This brings us to our final division, which is found in verse 30, about what a virtuous woman should set her heart on. The world is so focused on outward beauty, but inward beauty is the only thing that will never fade. What do you set your heart on? Are you putting on the characteristics of a virtuous woman whose heart is set on the Lord? Or are you trying to cover that up by focusing more on outward beauty? 1 Samuel 16:7 tells us, "But the Lord said to Samuel, "Do not consider his appearance or his height, for I have rejected him. The Lord does not look at the things people look at. People look at the outward appearance, but the Lord looks at the heart." What would God see if He were to look at your heart? Set your heart on the Lord and all of the characteristics of a virtuous woman will follow.

Go-Go Bananas Monkey Bread

This fun version of monkey bread is sure to make your family "go-go bananas" over this sweet dish.

Ingredients:

1 cup Sugar

6 teaspoons Cinnamon

½ cup Butter

1 cup Brown Sugar

3 cans Jumbo Refrigerated Biscuits (8 count)

4 Bananas

1½ cups Chopped Walnuts (optional)

Preheat oven to 350 degrees.

In a small bowl, mix together the sugar and cinnamon, then set it aside. In a saucepan over low heat, melt the butter and brown sugar until combined. Prepare a Bundt pan with cooking spray, unwrap the biscuits, and cut the bananas into small slices. Take the biscuit and press it out with your fingers. In the middle, place 2 or 3 banana slices and sprinkle ½ teaspoon of the cinnamon sugar; fold the biscuit, press the sides together, and roll into a ball. Roll the ball in the cinnamon sugar mix. Sprinkle ½ cup walnuts into the Bundt pan and start placing the prepared balls in the pan. Fit as many as you can into the bottom. Continue to layer by sprinkling ½ cup of walnuts on top, half of the cinnamon sugar mixture, then ½ cup sliced bananas, and then pour half of the brown sugar/butter mixture over the top. Prepare the second layer of balls, placing as many as you can fit into the pan. Sprinkle over the top the last ½ cup of walnuts, the second half of the cinnamon sugar, and the rest of the brown sugar mixture.

Bake in the oven for 45 minutes. Let cool for 5 minutes and then invert onto a plate. Note: If your Bundt pan is almost full, make sure you put it on top of a cookie sheet when you bake it to prevent the juices from overflowing onto your oven.

O Lord, be gracious to us;
We have waited for You. Be
their arm every morning,
Our salvation also in the
time of trouble.

~ Isaiah 33:2

LET GO AND LET GOD

The Lord said to him, "Who gave human beings their mouths? Who makes them deaf or mute? Who gives them sight or makes them blind? Is it not I, the Lord? Now go; I will help you speak and will teach you what to say."

~ Exodus 4:11–12

Have you ever been in a situation where you had an opportunity to witness to someone, but were too afraid to say anything? Moses was. When God came to him in a burning bush asking him to lead His people out of Egypt, Moses's response was that he was wrong for the job because he was slow of speech—or in other words, he was scared. However, God never chooses the wrong person to speak for Him. His response to Moses was that He would be there with Moses every step of the way. God puts these same opportunities in our lives every day, but often we miss them because we are too scared or embarrassed.

Witnessing to others is not an easy thing to do: that's why we need God's help. He never presents us with an opportunity to witness and then leaves us there to speak on our own. If you are afraid of what the response will be, just remember 1 John 4:18–19, "There is no fear in love. But perfect love drives out fear, because fear has to do with punishment. The one who fears is not made perfect in love. We love because He first loved us." Our love for Jesus Christ will drive out that fear as soon as we start speaking. God will give us the right words to say. He is the One speaking through us so even if we hear it one way, He will allow others to hear it the way He wants it to be heard.

We are going to be held accountable for the people we choose not to witness to when given the opportunity. Ezekiel 33:6 says, "But if the watchman sees the sword coming and does not blow the trumpet to warn the people and the sword comes and takes someone's life, that person's life will be taken because of their sin, but I will hold the watchman account-able for their blood." As Christians, we know the fate of unbelievers, but if we choose not to share the way of salvation to them, God will hold us accountable for not taking that opportunity. God says in 2 Peter 3:9 that He doesn't want anyone to perish; therefore we need to have the same mindset as our Lord and Savior. Be on the lookout daily for the opportunity to share the gospel with someone; even if they don't accept it, you have done your duty to plant a seed which could one day lead them to salvation.

EASY CHILAQUILES

I love authentic chilaquiles. However, I found it a little time-consuming making everything from

scratch, so this is my Americanized semi-homemade version of chilaquiles.

INGREDIENTS:

13 ounces thick
Tortilla Chips

6 cups or 48 ounces of
Salsa Verde Green Sauce
(I like to use La Victoria
Thick 'N' Chunky Salsa
Verde Medium)

1 cup Yellow Onion,
chopped

1½ cups Monterey Jack
Cheese, shredded

Preheat the oven to 350 degrees.

In a large bowl, mix the salsa verde and onions together. Place the tortilla chips in a 9" x 13" Pyrex dish and pour the salsa verde mixture over the top.

Bake for 20 minutes, take out of the oven, and sprinkle the cheese over the top and bake for another 10 minutes. Serve with toppings such as fried or scrambled eggs (depending on if you like the yolk—I like it yolky!), sour cream, cilantro, and salsa.

No Such Thing as a Secret

Nothing in all creation is hidden from God's sight. Everything is uncovered and laid bare before the eyes of him to whom we must give account.

~ Hebrews 4:13

Nothing is hidden from the eyes of God. He sees and knows everything we do. Why is it we think that we can get away with sin? We may think that by not acting upon a thought makes it okay or that if we do something out of the sight of others that it doesn't count as a sin. Wrong. With God there are no secrets, and ultimately we will be held accountable for every thought, word, and action that we take.

In 2 Samuel 11 we read the famous story about David and Bathsheba, how he lusted after her even though she was a married woman, committed adultery, and had her obedient husband, Uriah, killed in battle. David thought that he could get away with it if Uriah's death looked like an accident, and that it would look as if he was doing the pregnant Bathsheba a great service by taking her as his wife. Everything went according to plan and it seemed like David was in the clear, but he forgot the One who was watching—God. The Lord had been watching, and He sent Nathan to confront David, as we see in 2 Samuel 12:12–13a: "You did it in secret, but I will do this thing in broad daylight before all Israel." Then David said to Nathan, 'I have sinned against the Lord.'"

We need to be very careful about thinking we can get away with sin. There will be consequences for every decision we make. In David's case, the Lord's punishment for his murder and adultery was allowing his and Bathsheba's firstborn child to become ill and die, as well as allowing strife within his family for the remainder of his life. There will come a day when we will sit at the foot of God's throne giving an account of everything we did and everything we didn't do.

When you feel like you are on the brink of sinning—stop and pray. Ask the Lord to help you. Ask Jesus to intervene on your behalf to stop you from sinning or continuing to sin. Hebrews 7:25 declares, "Therefore He is able to save completely those who come to God through Him, because He always lives to intercede for them." Instead of hiding from God, take the opportunity to grow closer to Him by entrusting Him with your secrets and allowing God to transform your mind in a way that is pleasing in His sight.

PEANUT BUTTER FRENCH TOAST SANDWICHES

My dad is a huge fan of peanut butter sandwiches, so I thought how could I incorporate his (and my)

love of peanut butter into a breakfast dish? And then it came to me . . . stuffed Peanut Butter French

toast sandwiches.

INGREDIENTS:

4 Eggs

1 cup Whole Milk

1 teaspoon Cinnamon

½ teaspoon Maple Syrup Extract

½ teaspoon Vanilla

10 slices of Texas Toast Bread

½ cup Creamy or Chunky Peanut Butter

2 tablespoons Honey

6 tablespoons Cream Cheese, at room temperature

Preheat the oven to 350 degrees.

In a large bowl, whisk together the eggs, milk, cinnamon, maple, and vanilla extracts. In a separate small bowl, beat the peanut butter, honey, and cream cheese together until smooth. Take one slice of bread and spread about 3 tablespoons of the peanut butter mixture onto it, be generous and then top with another slice, making a sandwich. Repeat until you have 5 sandwiches.

Lightly grease a griddle with cooking spray and heat to 325 degrees. Take one of the peanut butter sandwiches and dip it into the egg mixture, making sure to coat each side while keeping the sandwich intact. Place sandwiches onto the hot griddle and cook until golden brown for 2 minutes, then flip and cook on the other side. While cooking, take a spatula and smash the sandwich down. Transfer onto a baking sheet. Repeat with all of the sandwiches until they are all on the sheet and then bake in the oven for 10 minutes. Makes 5 peanut butter French toast sandwiches; you can serve them with homemade maple syrup, butter, and a little powdered sugar sifted on top.

NOTES:

_____
_____
_____
_____
_____
_____
_____
_____
_____
_____
_____
_____
_____
_____
_____
_____
_____
_____
_____
_____
_____
_____
_____

GO AND TELL

The angel said to the women, "Do not be afraid, for I know that you are looking for Jesus, who was crucified. He is not here; he has risen, just as he said. Come and see the place where he lay. Then go quickly and tell his disciples: 'He has risen from the dead and is going ahead of you into Galilee. There you will see him.' Now I have told you." So the women hurried away from the tomb, afraid yet filled with joy, and ran to tell his disciples.

~ Matthew 28:5–8

These women were chosen by God to be the first witnesses of Christ's resurrection. It is interesting because in that day and age, women were not respected or regarded as they are now. They did not have a voice in their society, yet God chose them to be His voice in bringing His disciples the good news. The women in these passages were the two Marys: Mary Magdalene and Mary the mother of James. God used these two women, who were viewed by the world at their time as weak and insignificant, to be the first eye-witnesses and the first missionaries to tell others about how Christ defeated death, providing salvation to all who believe in Him.

Imagine a cool, crisp morning, still a little dark out, as these two Marys walk silently and somberly side by side to the tomb of their Lord and Savior. Only three days before, they had watched from afar as Jesus was nailed to the cross; at the moment of His death it was as if their hearts had been wrenched out of their chest, and they are still mourning the loss of their Master. As they approach His tomb, that feeling slowly starts to well up inside them again, but it is interrupted by a great earthquake. They stumble to the ground; when they look up, they see a piercing light, one so bright that they have to shield their eyes, and a creature so magnificent that it can only be an angel. In a strong voice, the angel tells them not to be afraid, that he knows they are looking for Jesus, but Jesus is not there; He is risen! Those were the only three words that rang through their minds as they both ran to tell the disciples: "He is risen!"

Do you have that same excitement about telling the good news about Jesus today? The Marys didn't casually walk to tell others about Jesus' resurrection: they ran at full speed; nothing could slow them down. After Jesus appeared to the disciples, He told them, in Mark 16:15b, "Go into all the world and preach the gospel to all creation." His command is simply to go and tell, not one or two people, but as many people as you come into contact with. Go and tell others with boldness and with excitement, just as the Marys did. He is risen!

BAKED CHEESY GRITS

One of my favorite memories is the time my Dad and I went to Florida to see the Superbowl. While we were down there, I met a woman named Cindy who had the same love of grits that I do. This is one of her famous grits recipes that she was gracious enough to give me.

INGREDIENTS:

6 cups water

2¼ teaspoons Salt

2 cups Yellow Grits (Not instant or quick; preferably stone ground)

½ cup Unsalted Butter

½ teaspoon Black Pepper

8 ounces Sharp Cheddar Cheese, grated

3 large Eggs

1 cup Whole Milk

Put oven rack in the middle and preheat the oven to 350 degrees.

Bring water and ¾ teaspoon salt to a boil in a 4-quart saucepan. Add grits in a slow stream, stirring constantly. Reduce heat to low, stirring frequently to avoid sticking, until very thick for about 20 minutes.

Add butter, pepper, cheese, and remaining salt; stir until butter and cheese are melted. Lightly beat eggs and milk in a small bowl, then stir into grits until combined.

Pour into an ungreased 8" square baking dish and bake until set and lightly browned: about one hour. Let cool for 15 minutes before serving. Makes 8 servings.

LET THE MORNING BRING ME
WORD OF YOUR UNFAILING LOVE,
FOR I HAVE PUT MY TRUST IN YOU.
SHOW ME THE WAY I SHOULD GO,
FOR TO YOU I ENTRUST MY LIFE.

~ PSALM 143:8 NIV

PROMISES, PROMISES

And she made a vow, saying, "Lord Almighty, if you will only look on your servant's misery and remember me, and not forget your servant but give her a son, then I will give him to the Lord for all the days of his life, and no razor will ever be used on his head."

~ 1 Samuel 1:11

God does not take promises lightly, and neither should we. It's so easy to make a promise to God when we want something—"Lord, I promise to do this" or "Lord, I promise to give that." Every promise that God has made He has kept; can we say the same? If we don't keep our promises to the Lord then we are actually lying to Him, and Proverbs 12:22 says, "The Lord detests lying lips, but he delights in people who are trustworthy."

Hannah was barren. She could not conceive a child, but as we see in our verse she begged God, promising that if He blessed her with a son, she would give her son back to Him in service. God blessed her with a son named Samuel and so, as soon as Hannah was done weaning Samuel, she gave him over to live with Eli the prophet, where he would be raised to serve and prophesy for the Lord. Hannah kept her promise; she was prepared to dedicate her son fully to God for the rest of his life.

When making a promise to God, make sure you are prepared to fulfill that promise. We need to be careful not to give empty promises to the One who saved us. Any vow that we make to God we need to fulfill; if we don't, then we are sinning against Him. Deuteronomy 23:21–23 tells us,

"If you make a vow to the Lord your God, do not be slow to pay it, for the Lord your God will certainly demand it of you and you will be guilty of sin. But if you refrain from making a vow, you will not be guilty. Whatever your lips utter you must be sure to do, because you made your vow freely to the Lord your God with your own mouth."

Prayerfully consider the promises that you make to both God and your family, and be sure that they are not done in haste. If you can't keep your promises, then refrain from them altogether. This will not only show that you respect what a promise is, but it will keep you from sinning in the sight of your family and against your Savior.

SPICED SOUR CREAM COFFEE CAKE

Everyone loves a good coffee cake recipe, and this one is packed full of nuts and spices.

INGREDIENTS:

1½ cups Sour Cream

1 teaspoon Baking Soda

3 cups All-Purpose Flour

2 teaspoons Baking Powder

1½ teaspoons Salt

1 teaspoon Ground Nutmeg

1 teaspoon Cinnamon

¼ teaspoon Ground Cloves

1 cup Unsalted Butter, at room temperature

1¾ cups Sugar

3 large Eggs

1 teaspoon Vanilla

NUT MIXTURE:

1 cup Pecans, roughly chopped

⅓ cup Sliced Almonds

3 tablespoons Granulated Sugar

3 tablespoons Brown Sugar

½ teaspoon Cinnamon

Preheat oven to 350 degrees.

In a small bowl, stir together sour cream and baking soda, let sit for about an hour. For the nut mixture, stir together all of the ingredients in a small bowl. Set aside. To make the batter, whisk together flour, baking powder, salt, nutmeg, cinnamon, and cloves in a large bowl. With an electric mixer, beat in the butter for about 2 minutes. Slowly mix in the sugar. Beat in the eggs and vanilla, adding one egg at a time. Finally mix in the sour cream that had been set aside. Mixture will be thick, but smooth.

In a well-greased Bundt cake pan or deep-dish pie pan, pour in half of the batter and smooth it out with a spoon. Sprinkle half of the nut mixture evenly over the batter. Repeat that process ending with the nut mixture again and smoothing it all out.

Bake for 50 minutes or until a knife inserted into the center comes out clean. Let cool for 25 to 30 minutes. Place a cooling rack on the top of the cake and invert the cake, carefully lifting the pan off. Let cool and serve.

THE LAWS OF LOVE

Love is patient, love is kind. It does not envy, it does not boast, it is not proud. It does not dishonor others, it is not self-seeking, it is not easily angered, it keeps no record of wrongs. Love does not delight in evil but rejoices with the truth. It always protects, always trusts, always hopes, always perseveres.

~ 1 Corinthians 13:4–7

These verses are some of the most famous Bible verses on love, and are known by both Christians and non-Christians alike. Though you normally hear them recited during a wedding ceremony, they don't only apply to a marital relationship, but also in your relationship with your family, friends, and most importantly, with Jesus. If we really delve into the attributes of love that these verses describe, we will begin to see what true love is all about.

True love is rarely seen in our world today. Instead we see failed marriages, love tainted by worldly ambitions, and love focused only on the physical. Our only example of a perfect, true love is from Jesus Christ, who not only showed us this love through His words but through His actions, sacrificing Himself as the atonement for our sins. He loved us so much that He died to save us from an eternal fate of suffering; by rising from the dead he defeated death so that we don't have to face it. Jesus had every attribute listed in these verses; as followers of Christ, we need to strive to be more like our Savior.

The laws of His perfect love show us how to act inwardly and outwardly. Love is patient. By showing patience in the relationships that we have, we show our trust in God's plan for our lives. He is in control and everything is perfect in His timing. Love is kind. Jesus had people who hated Him, yet He was kind even toward them. Love does not envy. This can be a hard one, especially for us women, but we should be happy and excited for our friends and family when they are blessed. Do not boast or be prideful, because James 4:6 tells us, "But he gives us more grace. That is why Scripture says: 'God opposes the proud but shows favor to the humble.'"

Dishonoring others can be done in many ways, but one of the most common ways is through gossip and by putting others down for personal gain. Instead, strive to be a servant to others. Slow to anger. Pick and choose your battles and words wisely, because they can hurt more than you know. Keep no record of wrongs. The old self and old lifestyle has passed away, but you are a new creation, so keep your eyes on the cross, not on the scenery behind it. Be thankful and rejoice in God's truth. Never delight when your neighbor stumbles, instead help them up and lead them in love.

The final laws of love are what keep love strong. Try replacing the word love with God in this passage: God always protects us, God always trusts in us, God always hopes in us, and God always perseveres for us, even when we have given up. True love is when God is at the center.

ONION TART

Onion Tart may not sound appealing, but if you can get past the name it's absolutely amazing! My husband and I first tried it in Strasbourg, France, where they are known for their mouthwatering onion pies. After a lot of trial and error, I came up with this recipe that replicates what we tasted in Strasbourg, and I know you will love it!

INGREDIENTS:

¼ cup Oil

4 Sweet Onions, Sliced

7 slices Thick Bacon

4 Eggs

⅓ cup Cream

⅓ cup Whole Milk

½ teaspoon Salt

½ teaspoon Pepper

¼ teaspoon Nutmeg

Preheat the oven to 350 degrees.

Prepare the crust using the Savory Crust recipe on page 133. Press into a tart dish or pie dish; let cool in refrigerator.

Pour the oil into a large skillet and set over medium-low heat. Add the sliced onions and 3 strips of bacon; sauté until the onions are caramelized and soft. Dice the remaining 4 strips of bacon into small pieces and cook in a separate small saucepan until crispy. Once the onions start to caramelize, take out the 3 full strips of bacon and discard (or eat!). Add the crispy bacon pieces to the caramelized onions, making sure not to pour in the bacon grease as well; stir to combine and then remove from the heat. In a medium bowl, whisk together the eggs, cream, milk, salt, pepper, and nutmeg. Add the onions to the milk mixture, stir to combine, and pour into the prepared pie dish.

Bake for an hour or until the middle no longer jiggles and the top is lightly browned. Cool for about 20 minutes before serving. Note: If the top starts to burn, cover loosely with a piece of foil.

ACTIONS SPEAK LOUDER THAN WORDS

Dear children, let us not love with words or speech
but with actions and in truth.

~ 1 John 3:18

Have you ever heard the phrase, "Actions speak louder than words?" It's true. You can talk all you want, but it's not until there is a change in your actions that people begin to believe it's true. God's love is a radical transformation of lifestyle. When Christ is in our lives, everything is made new—our speech, our thoughts, our attitudes, and our behavior. His truth now shines through our every word. This is why we not only need to show Christ's love to others with our words, but also with our actions.

The change in the Apostle Paul's life was radical. He was infamous for persecuting Christians in Jerusalem, until one day God changed Paul's life forever and called him into God's service. When people heard Paul preaching about Jesus they were amazed, as we see in Acts 9:21-22: "All those who heard him were astonished and asked, 'Isn't he the man who raised havoc in Jerusalem among those who call on this name? And hasn't he come here to take them as prisoners to the chief priests?' Yet Saul grew more and more powerful and baffled the Jews living in Damascus by proving that Jesus is the Messiah." The drastic change in Paul's life was what made people want to listen to what he had to say. From that point on, Paul's actions would speak louder than his words.

Our actions matter in our witness for Christ. We contradict ourselves when we say one thing yet act entirely different. We can't claim Christianity but live like the rest of the world. There needs to be a drastic difference between our actions and the world's: our words are not enough. Jesus is our Truth; we need to base our actions around His words. As 1 John 2:6 says, "Whoever claims to live in him must live as Jesus did." Of course we are all sinners who fall short of His glory, so we don't have to be perfect, but we do have to strive for His perfection.

RED VELVET SCONES WITH SWEET CREAM CHEESE DRIZZLE

My mom, sister, and I love going to tea houses. Through the years, we've always had our own tea parties too. These scones are so festive for an afternoon tea.

INGREDIENTS:

2 cups Flour

4 teaspoons Baking Powder

¾ teaspoon Salt

⅓ cup Sugar

¼ cup Unsweetened Cocoa Powder

4 tablespoons Butter

2 tablespoons Shortening

¾ cup Sour Cream

1 Egg

2 teaspoons Red Food Coloring

FROSTING:

1½ cups Powdered Sugar

4 tablespoons Milk

1 teaspoon Vanilla

4 ounces Cream Cheese, room temperature

Preheat the oven to 375 degrees.

In a large mixing bowl, combine the flour, baking powder, salt, sugar, and cocoa powder. Add the shortening and cut in the butter. In a separate small bowl, whisk together the sour cream and egg, then pour it into the dry ingredient mix. Add the food coloring. Put on plastic disposable kitchen gloves to refrain from getting food coloring on your hands, and then knead the ingredients together until fully combined.

On a floured surface, roll dough out and cut with your choice of cookie cutter (see note below). Place on a cookie sheet lined with parchment paper and bake for 15 minutes. Let cool for about 10 minutes and then drizzle with cream cheese frosting.

SWEET CREAM CHEESE FROSTING:

With an electric hand mixer, blend all ingredients together until smooth.

Note: To keep your counters from getting stained, lay a couple pieces of plastic wrap down over your countertop, flour them, and roll the dough out on the plastic wrap. It makes for easy clean up too!

I, Jesus, have sent my angel to testify to you these things in the churches. I am the Root and the Offspring of David, the Bright and Morning Star.

~ Revelation 22:16

GREEN WITH ENVY

A heart at peace gives life to the body, but envy rots the bones.

~ Proverbs 14:30

We have all been blessed differently in our lives—some people have more, and some have less. Our culture has become so egotistical that many people burn with envy for whatever someone else has. It is a twisted "keeping up with the Joneses" point of view where jealousy reigns in the heart. But if you don't give them up to the Lord quickly, jealousy and envy become more than just emotions of resentment. As we see in our verse, envy rots the bones; it slowly eats away at you until the greed completely consumes your being.

Envy, at its hollow heart, is self-seeking and plants a seed of hatred. James 3:16 tells us, "For where you have envy and selfish ambition, there you find disorder and every evil practice." The results of envy can be devastating. It opens a door to many other types of sin, as we see in Romans 1:29: "They have become filled with every kind of wickedness, evil, greed and depravity. They are full of envy, murder, strife, deceit and malice. They are gossips." The moment you let envy start to dwell in your mind is the moment it becomes sinful. In Genesis 4, we see how envy consumed Cain to the point where he killed his brother Abel because Abel's offering to God was pleasing and Cain's was not.

So how are we to stop envy at its root? The answer is we don't, God does. Immediately ask Jesus for peace when you feel that tinge of envy creeping up, and He will give you the peace you need to overcome this emotion. Philippians 4:7 says, "And the peace of God, which transcends all understanding, will guard your hearts and your minds in Christ Jesus." Be thankful for the things the Lord has given you because "every good and perfect gift is from above" (James 1:17a). When we are content with what God has given us, we will be able to serve Him more fully and wholeheartedly. We have all been blessed with different responsibilities and duties in this life, so let us serve the Lord with what He has given to us and not be envious of what He hasn't.

NOTES:

THREE PEPPER FRITTATA

A frittata is similar to an omelet, but it serves more than one person. This is a veggie frittata with a little kick to it.

INGREDIENTS:

6 eggs, beaten

1 ounce Parmesan Cheese

½ teaspoon Pepper

1 tablespoon Butter

½ cup Yellow Bell Peppers, chopped

½ cup Red Bell Peppers, chopped

1 Jalapeño Pepper, thinly chopped

½ cup Swiss Cheese, Shredded

Preheat the oven to Broil.

In a medium bowl, whisk together the eggs, parmesan cheese, and pepper. In a 12" non-stick oven safe skillet over low heat, melt the butter. Add the bell peppers and chopped jalapeno, turn the heat up to medium and sauté for about 5 minutes. Pour the egg mixture into the skillet and stir.

Cook without stirring for 4 minutes or until the frittata starts to cook through to the top; immediately transfer to the oven to broil for about 4 minutes until lightly browned and fluffy. Open the oven, sprinkle the Swiss cheese evenly onto the frittata, and broil for 1 more minute. Remove from the pan onto a plate and serve. Makes 6 to 8 servings.

MISERY LOVES COMPANY

Do not be misled: "Bad company corrupts good character."
~ 1 Corinthians 15:33

We have all heard the saying, "Misery loves company." It's the idea that if someone is unhappy, they want everyone else around them to be unhappy as well. The same thing applies to the friends we surround ourselves with. If we allow people into our lives who are in some way a bad influence, don't be fooled into thinking that you can change them. Yes, they can be influenced by your behavior and actions, however, only God can change their hearts—if they are willing. To surround yourself with bad company gives Satan a foothold into your life. He will constantly be trying to pull your character down to match theirs.

This doesn't necessarily mean that you need to completely cut off contact; however, it's probably not wise to be hanging out with them on a regular basis. For example, if you believe that the best way to witness to your wayward friends is by accompanying them in their controversial activities, think again. Not only are you putting yourself in temptation's way, but you could also be causing others around you to stumble in the process. Another mistake is thinking that you are strong enough to handle any temptation Satan throws at you. Matthew 26:41 tells us, "Watch and pray so that you will not fall into temptation. The spirit is willing, but the flesh is weak."

The best way to handle a bad friendship is, first, keep them in your prayers. Ask God to soften their hearts and to show them the error of their ways. Second, gently be honest with them, not in an "I'm-better-than-you" way, but in a way that expresses your genuine concern and disagreement with their actions. I have always admired my sister, because whenever she disagreed with the way her friends would act, she would always tell them straightaway but in a kind and godly manner. This always caused her friends to respect my sister even more than they did before. That is what a genuine friend in Christ is. Most importantly, pray for God to give you discernment on how to handle your friendships, asking that He will allow you to be a light in their lives.

STRAWBERRY LEMONADE

Strawberry lemonade seems to be a hit with everyone, and this recipe is oh-so-yummy.

INGREDIENTS:

1 pound Fresh Strawberries, sliced (about 3 cups)

1 cup Fresh Lemon Juice (5 lemons)

1 cup Sugar

1 teaspoon Lemon Zest

1 tablespoon Mint, finely chopped (optional)

4 cups Water

Ice

In a medium skillet, cook the strawberries, ¾ cup sugar, and lemon zest until sugar is dissolved into syrup and the strawberries are tender. Emulsify with a blending stick. Pour into a large pitcher or punch bowl. Mix in the lemon juice, ¼ cup sugar, mint, water, and ice. Serve in glasses with a sugared rim and a lemon slice on top. Serves 6 to 8 people.

A Word to the Wise

Now, Lord my God, you have made your servant king in place of my father David. But I am only a little child and do not know how to carry out my duties. Your servant is here among the people you have chosen, a great people, too numerous to count or number. So give your servant a discerning heart to govern your people and to distinguish between right and wrong. For who is able to govern this great people of yours?

~ 1 Kings 3:7–9

If you could ask for one thing from the Lord and He would give it to you, what would you ask for? Solomon was given this rare opportunity at the age of 19 when he became king. He could have anything he wanted, but unlike most people, he didn't ask for wealth or a life of grandeur. Instead, Solomon asked for wisdom. God was pleased by Solomon's request because he could have asked for a million things that he wanted, but instead he asked for something that he absolutely needed. God not only made him the wisest man on earth, but He also blessed him above and beyond anything he could've imagined.

This is absolutely something we can apply to our prayer life. We often pray for things we want instead of praying for the things we need. When Solomon asked for wisdom, his heart was focused on how he could glorify God. The next time you start to pray about something you want, stop and think about who it will bring glory to. Solomon needed wisdom in order to govern God's people; he recognized that his youth and lack of experience was a weakness, so that's where Solomon asked

God to fill him. He wanted to bring glory to God's kingdom by being a wise king to His people.

There are so many worldly things that we could pray for, but none of them are things that truly matter. Worldly desires will always leave us wanting more; they will never truly satisfy us. In praying for things we need, we put more trust in God to provide for us. Matthew 6:33 says, "But seek first His kingdom and His righteousness, and all these things will be given to you as well." Our prayers need to be Christ-centered instead of self-centered. Every need that God provides is a blessing, and every want He gives is a gift.

BANANA BREAD

My in-laws eat their banana bread with cream cheese and butter on top, and it is so yummy. This bread is super moist and great without any toppings, but try serving it with cream cheese; your family will love it.

INGREDIENTS:

1¾ All-Purpose Flour

1½ teaspoons Baking Soda

¾ teaspoon Salt

3 large Eggs

1½ cups Sugar

1 teaspoon Vanilla

3 large ripe Bananas, mashed

1 eight-ounce Cream Cheese, softened

¾ cup Vegetable Oil

Preheat oven to 350 degrees.

In a small bowl, whisk together the flour, baking soda, and salt. In a separate large bowl, whisk together the eggs, sugar, vanilla, bananas, cream cheese, and oil. Slowly stir in the flour mixture into the banana mixture until combined. Spray a 9" x 5" x 3" loaf pan with cooking spray and pour the batter into the prepared pan.

Bake for an hour or until a toothpick inserted into the middle of the bread comes out clean. If the bread gets too brown on the top, loosely cover it with a piece of foil and let it continue to bake. Let cool in pan for about 15 minutes before you release the bread onto a wire rack to cool. Note: You can substitute two small bread pans for one big pan. Bake for the same amount of time.

For behold, He who forms mountains, And creates the wind, Who declares to man what his thought is, And makes the morning darkness, Who treads the high places of the earth— The Lord God of hosts is His name.

~ Amos 4:13

_____

_____

_____

_____

_____

_____

_____

_____

_____

_____

_____

_____

_____

_____

_____

_____

_____

_____

_____

_____

_____

_____

STAY AWAKE!

Be on guard! Be alert! You do not know when that time will come. It's like a man going away: He leaves his house and puts his servants in charge, each with their assigned task, and tells the one at the door to keep watch. Therefore keep watch because you do not know when the owner of the house will come back—whether in the evening, or at midnight, or when the rooster crows, or at dawn. If he comes suddenly, do not let him find you sleeping. What I say to you, I say to everyone: "Watch!"

~ Mark 13:33–37

The biggest mistake someone can make is waiting to make a full commitment to the Lord. Many people say that they will wait till the end of their life to accept Jesus as their Savior, or that they will wait until they're married to fully serve Him. The truth is that only God knows when our time on this earth is up; we don't know what tomorrow holds. This is why waiting is futile; we need to live for Christ now! If we do this, then we will always be ready for the Lord's return. We won't have to worry if tomorrow is our last day, because we will have done all that we can do to serve Him.

The longer you wait to make a full commitment to Jesus, the harder it is going to get. There will always be something standing in your way; Satan will make sure of that. False teachers will mock us and say that Jesus will never return and that people have been talking about His return for thousands of years. Do not be led astray by this way of thinking. Jesus will return at a time that we won't expect; it may be in our lifetime or it may not be, but either way we want to be ready for it. 2 Peter 3:11–12a says, "Since everything will be destroyed in this way, what kind of people ought you to be? You ought to live holy and godly lives as you look forward to the day of God and speed its coming."

In our verses for today, Jesus tells a parable about a man leaving his house and putting his servants in charge. We are Jesus's servants; He has left us in charge until He returns again. How are you furthering your Father's work each day? Have you been sleeping instead of preparing for His return? Stay awake; be prepared! No one knows the time or hour of Jesus's return, so live each day thinking that today will be the day.

OVERNIGHT BREAKFAST QUICHE

My Aunt Nancy usually makes this quiche the day after Thanksgiving, and we all look forward to it;

it's so delicious!

INGREDIENTS:

6 to 10 slices White Soft Bread, with crusts trimmed off

3 cups Diced Ham

2 cups Sliced Mushrooms

1 cup Monterey Jack Cheese, grated

1 cup Sharp Cheddar Cheese, grated

1½ cups Milk

1 teaspoon Mustard (dry or prepared)

½ teaspoon Salt

½ teaspoon Pepper

8 Eggs

Lightly butter white bread on both sides (make sure butter is soft). Lay in bottom of 9" x 13" Pyrex dish. In a small bowl, toss the cheeses together. In two layers, sprinkle the ham on top of bread, then layer with mushrooms and cheese. Repeat. In a medium bowl, whisk together the milk, mustard, salt, and pepper. In a separate small bowl, lightly beat the 8 eggs and add to milk mixture. Pour evenly over the prepared Pyrex dish, cover with foil and put in the fridge overnight.

Bake for 45 minutes to 1 hour at 350 degrees. Cheese will be bubbly and slightly browned.

PRAYER WARRIORS

And pray in the Spirit on all occasions with all kinds of prayers and requests. With this in mind, be alert and always keep on praying for all the Lord's people. Pray also for me, that whenever I speak, words may be given me so that I will fearlessly make known the mystery of the gospel.

~ Ephesians 6:18–19

As Christian women, one of our strongest weapons is prayer. Prayer not only draws us closer to our Savior, but it also strengthens our fellow believers. One of the greatest gifts that accompany our salvation is having an open relationship with God through prayer. Without prayer, we miss out on the forgiveness that Jesus has to offer and the many blessings that He wants to abundantly bless us with. 1 Timothy 2:1–3 is the best example of why we pray: "I urge, then, first of all, that petitions, prayers, intercession and thanksgiving be made for all people—for kings and all those in authority, that we may live peaceful and quiet lives in all godliness and holiness. This is good, and pleases God our Savior" When should we pray? Anytime and anywhere, whether at home or at work, on the road, at a friend's house, working out, cooking, cleaning: you can pray whenever and wherever you want! A prayer is just talking to God, telling Him what's on your heart; it can be as long or as short as you'd like it to be. If you are unsure about how to start, A.C.T.S. is a wonderful guideline for prayer.

A is for Adoration—give praises to the Lord in any way you can think of. David gave adoration to God in Psalm 36:5: "Your love, Lord, reaches to the heavens, your faithfulness to the skies."

C is for Confession—it is extremely important to seek forgiveness from Jesus for the sins you have committed against Him. Don't be vague;

be specific, naming each one. 1 John 1:9 tells us, "If we confess our sins, He is faithful and just and will forgive us our sins and purify us from all unrighteousness."

T is for Thanksgiving—thank Him for your day, the food you are about to eat, the answers to prayers, and the ways He has blessed you. Thanking God for someone else's answered prayers are essential as well, because He is worthy of all praise.

Finally, S is for Supplication—ask Jesus for guidance, protection, comfort, healing, and anything that is on your heart that you need His help with, for yourself and for others. Sometimes God doesn't answer a prayer right away, but that doesn't mean you should stop praying. He will always give us an answer, even if it is through silence, but it will be in His timing, not ours. Always persevere and always be steadfast in your faith in Jesus when you pray. Take time each day to build your relationship with Jesus through prayer and remember the words of James 4:8a, "Come near to God and He will come near to you."

NOTES:

Mom's Blueberry Muffins

Whenever my mom would make these blueberry muffins, my sister and I would gobble them up! These will not last long after you make them!

Ingredients:

2 cups All-Purpose Flour

1½ cups Sugar

2 teaspoons Baking Powder

½ teaspoon Salt

½ cup Milk

½ cup Butter, melted and at room temperature

1 Egg, lightly beaten

1 teaspoon Vanilla

1½ cups Fresh or Frozen Blueberries (I prefer fresh)

Preheat oven to 400 degrees and lightly grease muffin tin with cooking spray.

In large bowl, stir together flour, sugar, baking powder, and salt. In a separate bowl, stir together milk, butter, egg, and vanilla until blended. Make a well in center of dry ingredients, pour the milk mixture into the well, and mix just until combined. Stir in blueberries. Spoon batter into prepared muffin tins using an ice cream scoop or something similar. Do not use any cupcake paper holders.

Bake 15 to 20 minutes until lightly browned; cool 5 minutes before removing from the tin. Makes 12 muffins.

Note: Do not double the batch, if you want to make more, start the batch over.

NOTES:

————————————
————————————
————————————
————————————
————————————
————————————
————————————
————————————
————————————
————————————
————————————
————————————
————————————
————————————
————————————
————————————
————————————
————————————
————————————
————————————
————————————

TRAINING FOR THE RACE

Do you not know that in a race all the runners run, but only one gets the prize? Run in such a way as to get the prize. Everyone who competes in the games goes into strict training. They do it to get a crown that will not last, but we do it to get a crown that will last forever. Therefore I do not run like someone running aimlessly; I do not fight like a boxer beating the air. No, I strike a blow to my body and make it my slave so that after I have preached to others, I myself will not be disqualified for the prize.

~ 1 Corinthians 9:24–27

If you have ever trained for a marathon, you know that it takes a lot of discipline. The training is strenuous and sometimes even unbearable! You have to discipline your mind to push harder and go farther each day. In comparison, our Christian walk is the marathon and the crown of service is our prize. As Christians, we have each been called by God to live a life of service to Him. Each calling is different, but we all strive towards the same goal. In order to accomplish our goal, we need to train ourselves up in righteousness and discipline our minds to think in the likeness of Christ.

The apostle Paul was a dedicated soldier of Christ; he lived and breathed to serve Him. It wasn't easy though; in order to get the crown of service it took dedication, endurance, and a lot of suffering. In verse 1:21 of his letter to the Philippians , Paul said, "For to me, to live is Christ and to die is gain." Paul made sure that as long as he was on this earth, his life would be lived solely for Christ. And if he died that would be a gain, because he would have completed his task that God had given him, and his reward would be to see his Savior face to face.

We are all born natural sinners, so without training and disciplining ourselves to live holy lives, we will always fall back into our sinful nature. In order to train ourselves up in righteousness we need to know the Bible intimately. 2 Timothy 3:16–17 says, "All Scripture is God-breathed and is useful for teaching, rebuking, correcting and training in righteousness, so that the servant of God may be thoroughly equipped for every good work." Just as water is necessary for runners in a race, so Scripture is our living water in our Christian walk.

To discipline our minds to think in the likeness of Christ, we have to have a daily relationship with Him. If we don't take time to know Him, how can we live our lives for Him? Romans 12:2 tells us, "Do not conform to the pattern of this world, but be transformed by the renewing of your mind. Then you will be able to test and approve what God's will is—his good, pleasing and perfect will." Through an active relationship with Christ, He will renew your mind to think more like Him and to see what is pleasing in His eyes.

After you have lived for Christ and He finally calls you home, just imagine Him saying to you those glorious words of Matthew 25:23, "Well done, good and faithful servant!" Wouldn't you want, at that moment, to lay your crowns of service at His feet? Living for Christ is worth the prize; just make sure that you train to win the crown for Him.

Traditional Strawberries 'n Cream

When I was 16 my family and I went on a trip to London to watch Wimbledon. I will never forget eating a bowl of this simple, classic London dish at the game.

Ingredients:

4 cups whole Strawberries, hulled

2 cups Heavy Cream

1 teaspoon Vanilla

2½ tablespoons Sugar

In a small bowl, whisk together the heavy cream, vanilla, and sugar. Place one cup of berries into 4 individual dishes or bowls and pour a half cup of the cream mixture over the berries and serve. This will make 4 servings.

THE LORD IS RIGHTEOUS IN
HER MIDST, HE WILL DO NO UN-
RIGHTEOUSNESS. EVERY MORN-
ING HE BRINGS HIS JUSTICE TO
LIGHT; HE NEVER FAILS.

~ ZEPHANIAH 3:5A

_____
_____
_____
_____
_____
_____
_____
_____
_____
_____
_____
_____
_____
_____
_____
_____
_____
_____
_____
_____
_____
_____

MONEY ≠ HAPPINESS

Those who want to get rich fall into temptation and a trap and into many foolish and harmful desires that plunge people into ruin and destruction. For the love of money is a root of all kinds of evil. Some people, eager for money, have wandered from the faith and pierced themselves with many griefs.

~ 1 Timothy 6:9–10

Wealth is a blessing and a privilege given to us by God. The moment it becomes a curse is when we start to view it as the source of our happiness. Our verse says that the love of money is a trap that many fall into. It causes us to lose sight of our Lord who ultimately is the One who gives and takes away. Money doesn't buy happiness, despite what our media depicts. There is nothing wrong with being blessed with wealth, but if we begin to live for money instead of living for Christ, we will fall into a lifestyle filled with grief.

As Christian women, we need to look at things with an eternal light, not getting caught up in the desires of this world. God will provide us with all that we need, and the more He blesses us with, the bigger our responsibility becomes. The moment we take our eyes off the eternal goal is the moment we will start to look for something to fulfill our temporal needs. Matthew 6:19–21 says, "Do not store up for yourselves treasures on earth, where moths and vermin destroy, and where thieves break in and steal. For where your treasure is, there your heart will be also." Ask yourself where your heart is today; if it isn't in the right place, ask Jesus to show you the things of this earth with an eternal light.

Jesus told us in Luke 12:48b, "From everyone who has been given much, much will be demanded; and from the one who has been entrusted with much, much more will be asked." If you have been given much by God, whether it is wealth or anything else, He expects you to use it for His glory. So many people fall into the trap of thinking that money equals happiness, but the empty chase after the love of money will never satisfy—because only Jesus can quench a thirsty heart. The more content we are with what He has given to us, the more we will see how fleeting the love of money is.

CROQUE-MONSIEUR SUB-SANDWICH

This is fun to serve for brunch. It's a Croque-Monsieur that serves a crowd; each person can simply slice off their own piece.

INGREDIENTS:

1 long baguette of Sourdough Bread

3 tablespoons Dijon Mustard

1 pound Black Forest Ham, sliced

3 cups Gruyere Cheese, shredded

BÉCHAMEL SAUCE

2 cups Whole Milk

2 tablespoons Unsalted Butter

3 tablespoons Flour

1 teaspoon Fresh Thyme, chopped

1 teaspoon Salt

½ teaspoon Pepper

½ cup Parmesan Cheese, grated

Preheat the oven to 400 degrees.

To make the béchamel sauce, heat the milk over medium heat in a small saucepan until hot, stirring occasionally, and then turn heat to low. In a separate small saucepan over medium heat, melt the butter, then whisk in the flour, stirring for about 2 minutes. Gradually add the milk to the flour mixture, whisking constantly. Add the thyme and whisk until the mixture gets thick and fully combined. Take off the heat and add the salt, pepper, and parmesan cheese, set aside.

Take the bread, slice a thin layer off the top, then slice the baguette in half horizontally, making it like a long sub sandwich. Spread the Dijon mustard on the inside of both slices, layer on the ham and then 2 cups of the Gruyere cheese. Press the sandwich together and place in the oven for 6 minutes or until the cheese is melted on the inside. Take out of the oven, turn the oven to Broil, and spread the béchamel sauce over the top of the sandwich. Sprinkle on the last 1 cup of Gruyere cheese and broil for another 5 to 6 minutes, until the top is bubbly and melted. Let cool for about 5 minutes before serving.

ALL EYES ON HIM

As Jesus and his disciples were on their way, he came to a village where a woman named Martha opened her home to him. She had a sister called Mary, who sat at the Lord's feet listening to what he said. But Martha was distracted by all the preparations that had to be made. She came to him and asked, "Lord, don't you care that my sister has left me to do the work by myself? Tell her to help me!" "Martha, Martha," the Lord answered, "you are worried and upset about many things, but few things are needed—or indeed only one. Mary has chosen what is better, and it will not be taken away from her."

~ Luke 10:38–42

Our lives are so busy; we are constantly on the go. If we don't slow our pace, we sometimes miss the opportunities that God presents to us. We can fill up our week with so many things that we forget to just stop and listen to what Jesus is saying to us, just like Martha did. I'm sure we have all been in Martha's shoes, busy preparing for an event, so distracted that we even overlooked what we were celebrating, which is the only thing that really matters. Jesus told her that only one thing is needed—her eyes on Him.

Mary sat quietly at the feet of Jesus listening to Him, letting His words pour into her life. She valued every single moment she had with Jesus and was willing to put everything else aside just to focus her attention on Him. Jesus tells us in John 12:26, "Whoever serves me must follow me; and where I am, my servant also will be. My Father will honor the one who serves me." Mary was honored by Jesus because she dropped everything to follow Him. Martha missed out on actually spending time with Jesus because her attention was on her sister and her priorities were elsewhere.

Sometimes it's not only the daily activities that we distract ourselves with, but also the people whom we choose to put above the Lord.

To be a servant of Christ is to make His work your first priority. Take time out of your day to stop and listen to Him. There are so many opportunities that we miss because we are too busy to look for them. We should always be on the lookout for ways to glorify God, even if it puts us out of our comfort zone. Ask God to help you to serve Him each day and to give you the strength to boldly speak His name. A servant always has her eyes on her Master; as long as we have our eyes on Him, He will surely honor us.

BELGIAN BENEDICT

This is a fun twist on eggs benedict. It's a lengthy process, but well worth the wait.

INGREDIENTS:

SAUCE:

4 tablespoons Cream

¼ cup Butter, softened

1 tablespoon White Vinegar

2 Eggs—yolks only

2 tablespoons Fresh Lemon Juice

⅛ teaspoon Sugar

⅛ teaspoon Salt

¼ teaspoon Cayenne Pepper

WAFFLES:

2 cups All-Purpose Flour

2 teaspoons Baking Powder

1 teaspoon Baking Soda

½ teaspoon Salt

3 tablespoons Granulated Sugar

2 cups Buttermilk

9 large Eggs

5 tablespoons Butter, melted

6 thick slices Canadian Bacon

¼ cup Brown Sugar

1 tablespoon Dijon Mustard

1 tablespoon Maple Syrup

HOLLANDAISE SAUCE:

Fill a saucepan with about 2 quarts of water and bring to a boil. Place a microwaveable bowl on top of the saucepan and turn the heat down to medium. Start adding all the ingredients, whisking constantly until hollandaise sauce starts to get thick: about 8 to 10 minutes. Cover and set aside.

WAFFLES

To make the waffles, combine the flour, baking powder, baking soda, salt, and granulated sugar in a medium bowl. In another small bowl, whisk together the buttermilk, 3 eggs, and the butter. Pour into the dry ingredients and stir until combined. Prepare your Belgian waffle iron and cook according to its instructions. Makes about 6 Belgian Waffles.

Preheat the oven to Broil. In a small bowl, mix together the brown sugar, Dijon mustard, and maple syrup. Take your Canadian bacon slices and coat both sides with the mix. Place the slices on a foil covered cookie sheet and broil for 4 minutes on each side. To prepare the poached eggs, fill a saucepan with about 2 quarts of water and bring to a boil. With a spoon, stir in a circular motion, creating a whirlpool effect and crack two eggs into the water. Let cook for 3 minutes and take out with a slotted spoon. Repeat the process 2 more times, until you have 6 poached eggs.

To assemble the Belgian Benedict, start with the waffle at the bottom, add the Canadian bacon on top, then the poached egg, and finish it off with the hollandaise sauce. Recipe makes about 6 Belgian Benedicts.

Working for Christ

Whatever you do, work at it with all your heart, as working for the Lord, not for human masters, since you know that you will receive an inheritance from the Lord as a reward. It is the Lord Christ you are serving.

~ Colossians 3:23–24

It's hard to always have a cheerful heart when you're working. By working, I mean anything from doing the laundry to going to a 9 to 5 job; but any work can become somewhat exhausting. The Lord tells us, however, to work at whatever we do as if we are working for Him. God is our true Master, and He wants His image to be reflected in every aspect of our work.

Our verse tells us that when Christ is the motivation behind our work, we will be rewarded; we will be blessed with an eternal reward for anything we do for the cause of Christ. When we work for Christ, it helps us live more fully for Him. Eventually, everything we do comes to be about the Lord.

Whether we are working for Christ at home or in an office, it's important not to complain about our job. You never know what the Lord is planning to bring about. As Ecclesiastes 3:22 says, "So I saw that there is nothing better for a person than to enjoy their work, because that is their lot. For who can bring them to see what will happen after them?" God has a plan for everything. You may be unemployed, unhappy at the job you are at, or just complaining about the work you have to do, but I guarantee that God has a purpose. His purpose may be to use you to touch someone else's life. Therefore, as Philippians 2:14 says, "Do everything without grumbling or arguing" so that you are always showing others that you are content with whatever work God has planned for you.

CHORIZO POTATO HASH

This hash is delicious. You can use it as a breakfast side or in breakfast burritos.

INGREDIENTS:

4 Idaho Potatoes, diced into small cubes and boiled in water for about 10 minutes (will be about 4 cups worth)

10 ounces Pork or Beef Chorizo

1 medium Yellow Onion, chopped

4 tablespoons Olive Oil

1 teaspoon Pepper

1 teaspoon Salt

In a large skillet, sauté the onions with the pepper and 2 tablespoons of olive oil until tender, about 5 minutes. Add the drained potato cubes, salt, and the remaining 2 tablespoons of olive oil and lightly stir together. The potatoes will be soft, so you don't want to mash them by stirring too much. Cook for about 15 minutes, stirring occasionally, until they start to get a golden brown hue.

At the same time, in a separate small skillet, cook the chorizo until thoroughly cooked and starting to brown, about 15 minutes. Set out a couple of paper towels on a plate and pour the chorizo out onto it so that the oil gets soaked up. After the chorizo has been drained of the oil, toss it in with the potato mixture. Stir lightly and cook for another 10 minutes or until it starts to crisp. Serves about 6 people.

For His anger is but for a moment, His favor is for life; Weeping may endure for a night, But joy comes in the morning.

~ Psalm 30:5

GROWING UP

Anyone who lives on milk, being still an infant, is not acquainted with the teaching about righteousness. But solid food is for the mature, who by constant use have trained themselves to distinguish good from evil.

~ Hebrews 5:13–14

Once we take that step of faith, committing our lives to living for Christ, it is time for us to grow up. How do we do that? We get to know who Jesus is. If you never spend time developing a relationship with Christ, you will never truly know Him. We know that through reading the Scripture and through daily prayer we get to know who Christ is on a deeper level, but our lives should also be reflecting what He teaches us.

1 Corinthians 13:11 says, "When I was a child, I talked like a child, I thought like a child, I reasoned like a child. When I became a man, I put the ways of childhood behind me." We have to take the next steps to grow into maturity with Christ by changing the way we speak, the way we think, and the way we reason.

One of the hardest things to do can be to think before we speak, but I would like to change this saying to "pray before we speak." Taming the tongue is a task that only Jesus can take on. Out of our mouths we gossip, slander, lie, curse, and deceive. James 1:26 tells us, "Those who consider themselves religious and yet do not keep a tight rein on their tongues deceive themselves, and their religion is worthless." It is impossible to control what we say on our own, so that's why giving it to the Lord can help us keep a tight rein on our tongues. The more we rely on God's words instead of our own, the more we will grow in Him through listening.

Normally, we aren't conscious of our thought—we just "think." However, when we allow the Holy Spirit to renew our minds, we give Him full reign to guide our lives and thoughts. By depending fully on the Holy Spirit, we no longer think through the eyes of the flesh but through the eyes of the Spirit. We will then start to see what pleases God, because we are no longer held captive by our fleshly minds but transformed by the Spirit. His love will begin to come out in our actions and words. Romans 8:5–6 says, "For those *who live* according to the flesh set their minds on the things of the flesh, but those who live according to the Spirit, the things of the Spirit. For to be carnally minded *is* death, but to be spiritually minded *is* life and peace."

What does it mean to "live according to the flesh"? It means that our own self-centered desires are the primary purpose and goal of our life. Before we knew Christ, our purpose was our self. We lived for ourselves alone—every man for himself. Now that we bear the Christian name, we should no longer live for ourselves, but for Christ. "I have been crucified with Christ; it is no longer I who live, but Christ lives in me; and the *life* which I now live in the flesh I live by faith in the Son of God, who loved me and gave Himself for me" (Galatians 2:20). Christ becomes the reason; Christ becomes the goal. He has a will and purpose for each of our lives here on earth, and our job is to follow Him. He is our reason for living, and serving Him is our goal.

Yoo-hoo Chocolate Pancakes with Homemade Whipped Cream

Forever a kid at heart, I have always loved Yoo-hoo. So here is my version of chocolate milk pancakes.

Ingredients:

2 cups Flour

2 tablespoons Sugar

2 teaspoons Baking Powder

1 teaspoon Baking Soda

¼ teaspoon Salt

1 teaspoon Vanilla

2 Eggs

2 cups plus 3 tablespoons Yoo-hoo (about three 6.5-ounce Yoo-hoo boxes)

¼ cup Butter, Melted

1 cup Semi-Sweet Chocolate Chips

1 cup Heavy Whipping Cream

1 tablespoon sugar

½ teaspoon Vanilla

To make the whipped topping, beat the heavy whipping cream, 3 tablespoons Yoo-hoo, sugar and vanilla in a medium bowl with an electric beater until firm peaks form, set aside.

In a large bowl, whisk together the first 5 ingredients. Add the vanilla, 2 cups Yoo-hoo, and egg; whisk until smooth. Last, add the melted butter and chocolate chips.

Over medium heat in a large skillet or a griddle, preheated to 325 degrees and sprayed with cooking spray, use a ¼ cup to ladle the batter for each pancake onto the griddle. Cook the pancake until it starts to bubble on the top, then flip it. These pancakes will be darker. Top with homemade Yoo-hoo whipped cream and serve. The recipe makes about 16 to 18 pancakes.

Pride Comes Before a Fall

Pride goes before destruction, a haughty spirit before a fall.

~ Proverbs 16:18

How easily we fall into pride. Pride takes God out of the picture and puts us into it. There is no accomplishment, reward, or promotion that we have gotten without God. He allows all of our successes in life, so when we start to praise ourselves for those successes instead of praising God, we fall into the trap of destruction. When we humble ourselves before God for everything He has done, He will honor us in everything we do.

Job stated in Job 1:21b, "The Lord gave and the Lord has taken away; may the name of the Lord be praised." Job was not proud; he was a humble man who walked with the Lord and was blessed with much. After everything was ripped away from Job in a matter of minutes, he still praised the Lord. Job recognized that everything he had was given to him by God; he had earned nothing by his own hand. He knew that God's will was greater than his own and that in all things, whether good or bad, God was worthy of his praise.

We will go through times in our life where everything seems to be going our way, but too often we forget who the Giver is. Psalm 10:4 says, "In his pride the wicked man does not seek Him; in all his thoughts there is no room for God." Pride puffs us up so much that we become self-reliant; we no longer seek after God's will, but our own. That is the moment we fall. So how do we prevent ourselves from our own self-destruction? We humble ourselves daily before the Lord and praise Him.

Think of all of the things God has given you, all of the small gifts that He blesses you with each day. Take this time to humble yourself before the Lord and praise Him for everything you can think of. Proverbs 29:23 says, "Pride brings a person low, but the lowly in spirit gain honor." After Job lost everything, God honored him for his faithfulness, humility, and praise by blessing Job with twice as much as he had before. If we are humble and praise God for the things He gives us, He will honor our name and keep us from falling into the shame of pride.

SAVORY CRUST

This is a savory crust recipe that I use for all my breakfast quiches and tarts.

INGREDIENTS:

1¼ cups Flour

¼ teaspoon Salt

¼ teaspoon Pepper

7 tablespoons Unsalted Butter, chilled and cut into cubes

1 or 2 tablespoons Cold Water

In a food processor, combine flour, salt, pepper, and butter; process until it resembles coarse crumbs. Add the water and pulse until it starts to come together, adding more water if needed. Roll the dough into a ball with your hands; wrap with plastic wrap and refrigerate for 1 hour before use.

Roll out chilled dough onto a floured surface, fit into a 9" tart pan or pie pan and chill until needed. Note: If you don't have a food processor, you can mix it by hand using a pastry blender or your hands. Just be careful not to over-mix.

THE BLAME GAME

*And we know that in all things God works for the good of those
who love Him, who have been called according to His purpose.*

~ Romans 8:28

When awful, inexplicable things happen in our lives, most of us, at one point or another, have blamed God. In those times it is difficult for us to think that God has an overarching plan that we will someday understand. Since we don't understand why God allows certain things to happen in our lives and in the world, we need to focus on the things that we can understand. By doing this, we will be able to see more clearly that God does have a purpose for everything.

In the beginning, God created a perfect, sinless world. It was not until Adam and Eve gave into Satan's temptation and disobeyed God that sin and death entered in. God did not put sin or death into our world; we did. 1 John 1:5 says, "This is the message we have heard from him and declare to you: God is light; in him there is no darkness at all." Ever since that perfect world was tainted with sin, every person's life now has an expiration date, and our world has been given into the hands of Satan, filling it with darkness.

Hebrews 2:14 shows us how Jesus, still being fully God, took the form of man just to save us from our sin: "Since the children have flesh and blood, He too shared in their humanity so that by His death He might break the power of him who holds the power of death—that is, the devil." Jesus is our light. Even though devastating, destructive things happen in life and we will all eventually die, Jesus is our Savior who has defeated the death that Satan put into this world through sin so that we can have eternal life with Him. When you blame God, you contradict His perfect character and miss the fact that His son Jesus Christ died for our mistake of letting sin into the perfect world He created for us.

As Christians, we are to love the Lord our God with all our heart, soul, strength, and mind (Luke 10:27). When we have a relationship with Jesus, we become God's children. As a parent looks after their children, so does God look after us. Why would God purposefully try to hurt us? He won't. In the limits of our human mind, however, we sometimes think that He does.

God is constantly trying to bring us closer to Him. We will suffer and go through hardships in this life because we no longer live in a perfect world, but when we do, we can choose to face them either by relying on God and trusting in His will for our life or by pointing the finger of blame. Please don't blame Jesus for some tragedy that sin or Satan has caused.

ENGLISH RASPBERRY TRIFLE

Oh how I love trifles! It is a beautiful dish that tastes just as delicious as it looks.

INGREDIENTS:

1 package Pound Cake (16 ounces), cut into 18 slices

2 five-ounce packages Instant Vanilla Pudding Mix

1 jar Raspberry Jam (18 ounces)

2 pints Fresh Raspberries

2 cups Heavy cream

2 tablespoons Sugar

1 teaspoon Vanilla

Prepare pudding according to package directions. In a small bowl, gently stir together the jam and 1½ pints of raspberries; set aside.

To start the layering, arrange one third of the sliced cake in the bottom of a clear trifle dish or large clear bowl. Spoon in one third of the pudding on top of the cake and spread evenly. On top of the pudding, spoon on one third of the raspberry mixture, spread evenly. Repeat the layering process two more times. Make sure that the layers are uniform, because you will see them from the outside of the bowl when finished. Chill in fridge.

Make the whipped cream in a small bowl by mixing the heavy cream, sugar, and vanilla with a hand blender until firm peaks start to form. Spread on the top of the layered trifle and place the remaining ½ pint of raspberries on top. This will serve 10 to 12 people.

But I will sing of Your power;

Yes, I will sing aloud of Your mercy in the morning;

For You have been my defense And refuge in the day of my trouble.

~ Psalm 59:16

NOTES:

_____

_____

_____

_____

_____

_____

_____

_____

_____

_____

_____

_____

_____

_____

_____

_____

_____

_____

_____

_____

_____

_____

THE VOICE OF REASON

And do not grieve the Holy Spirit of God, with whom you were sealed for the day of redemption.

~ Ephesians 4:30

What does it mean to grieve the Holy Spirit? When we accept Jesus as our Savior, the Holy Spirit comes into our lives and reigns in our hearts. He is our Voice of Reason; He guides us and speaks straight to the core of our being. To grieve the Holy Spirit is to ignore His guidance and direction. Each one of us unknowingly struggles with this each day. We have two choices when the temptation of sin arises: we can either follow the voice of the Holy Spirit or sinfully act out against Him. We do this through the things we read, what we watch, the words we say, the thoughts we have, or the actions that we take.

Song of Solomon 8:6 shows us how the seal of the Holy Spirit acts as our personal shield against sin. "Place me like a seal over your heart, like a seal on your arm; for love is as strong as death, its jealousy unyielding as the grave. It burns like blazing fire, like a mighty flame." Once we become one of Christ's children, we are sealed for the day of redemption. We will not have to endure the pain of eternal suffering; however, while we are on this earth we will have to deal with daily temptations. A seal is a symbol of ownership, when we claim ownership of Christ as our Savior, His Spirit claims ownership of us (NKJV Study Bible, 2007). We are able to fight against any temptation because the Holy Spirit is that seal. He fights for us and guides us to live for Christ rather than for our own selfish ambitions.

Each time we don't give into sin, the more aware we become. The Holy Spirit strengthens us so that we are more prepared to face it the next time it arises. 2 Timothy 1:7 tells us, "For the Spirit God gave us does not make us timid, but gives us power, love and self-discipline." When we choose to grieve the Holy Spirit, we are not only being blatantly disobedient, we are refusing to allow God to mold us into His image. By being sealed by the Holy Spirit we are allowing Him to be our defense against the temptation to fall into sin and therefore gaining strength against our adversary, so that we are prepared for whatever stumbling block he may put in our way.

HOMEMADE MAPLE SYRUP

If you are out of maple syrup or simply want to make your whole meal from scratch, this homemade maple syrup definitely hits the spot.

INGREDIENTS:

1 cup Sugar

1 cup Dark Brown Sugar

1 cup Water

2 tablespoons Butter

3 tablespoons Dark Corn Syrup

1 teaspoon Maple Extract

1 teaspoon Vanilla

In a saucepan over medium heat, combine the water and both sugars, stirring until the sugars dissolve. Add the butter, corn syrup, and maple and vanilla extracts.

Bring to a simmer for about 5 minutes or until it coats the back of a spoon. Pour into a 1 pint canning jar or Tupperware; store in the fridge. Reheat before use. Makes a little over a pint.

_____
_____
_____
_____
_____
_____
_____
_____
_____
_____
_____
_____
_____
_____
_____
_____
_____
_____
_____
_____
_____
_____

APPROVED BY GOD

For the appeal we make does not spring from error or impure motives, nor are we trying to trick you. On the contrary, we speak as those approved by God to be entrusted with the gospel. We are not trying to please people but God, who tests our hearts.

~ 1 Thessalonians 2:3–4

When we talk to others, whether it is to someone we are witnessing to or a friend who is asking for our advice, we need to keep in mind what our motive is. Our motive should always be to bring others the Word of God in a kind and honest manner that reflects the spirit of Jesus Christ. Colossians 3:17 sums up this attitude by saying, "And whatever you do, whether in word or deed, do it all in the name of the Lord Jesus, giving thanks to God the Father through Him." As Christian women, we have been entrusted with the gospel by God, so when we speak His Word, we need to keep in mind the One we are representing.

Telling someone what they want to hear can harm them more than it helps them. The truth may not be what they want to hear, but the truth spoken in love is what God has called us to speak. It is also important that we don't sugarcoat God's Word when we speak it; they are God's Words, not ours, therefore our truth needs to come directly from Scripture. 2 Corinthians 4:1–2 tells us, "Therefore, since through God's mercy we have this ministry, we do not lose heart. Rather, we have renounced secret and shameful ways; we do not use deception, nor do we distort the word of God. On the contrary, by setting forth the truth plainly we commend ourselves to everyone's conscience in the sight of God."

We need to have a sympathetic ear and be quick to listen, delivering the truth in love when a child or friend is in need. When we do this, God approves of our actions. He is the one who weighs our hearts, not anyone else. We will be held accountable by God for every word that comes out of our mouth, so let's make sure that with every word we are representing our Lord well. As 2 Timothy 2:15 says, "Do your best to present yourself to God as one approved, a worker who does not need to be ashamed and who correctly handles the word of truth."

Cinnamon Sugar Waffles with Fresh Strawberry Sauce

The cinnamon adds a little something special and makes this a sweet treat for breakfast.

Ingredients:

2 cups All-Purpose Flour

2 teaspoons Baking Powder

1 teaspoon Baking Soda

½ teaspoon Salt

3 tablespoons Sugar

½ tablespoon Cinnamon

2 cups Buttermilk

3 large Eggs

5 tablespoons Butter, melted

Strawberry Syrup:

1 pound Fresh Strawberries, sliced

1 cup sugar

1 teaspoon Cinnamon

¾ cup Water

1 tablespoon Lemon Juice

In a medium bowl, combine the flour, baking powder, baking soda, salt, sugar, and cinnamon. In a separate small bowl, whisk together the buttermilk, eggs, and butter. Pour into the dry ingredients and stir until combined.

Prepare your waffle iron and cook according to its instructions. Makes about 6 to 8 waffles.

Fresh Strawberry Syrup:

In a small saucepan over medium heat, add all of the ingredients and bring a boil , stirring until the mixture thickens. Emulsify with a blending stick. Pour over waffles and enjoy!

STEPPING OUT OF OUR COMFORT ZONE

This is what the Lord Almighty says: "Give careful thought to your ways. Go up into the mountains and bring down timber and build my house, so that I may take pleasure in it and be honored," says the Lord. "You expected much, but see, it turned out to be little. What you brought home, I blew away. Why?" declares the Lord Almighty. "Because of my house, which remains a ruin, while each of you is busy with your own house."

~ Haggai 1:7–9

Building up God's Kingdom requires us to step out of our comfort zone. Each day of our life on this earth is a gift from God. People generally don't realize this until something traumatic or detrimental happens in their lives, but why should we wait until this happens? God wants to use you to build His house today. We shouldn't be idly waiting around for something to wake us up to realize our purpose—God is our purpose! Galatians 2:20 says, "I have been crucified with Christ and I no longer live, but Christ lives in me. The life I now live in the body, I live by faith in the Son of God, who loved me and gave Himself for me." With each day that He graciously gives us, we should be living for Him. In order to do this we need to step out of the comfort of our own homes and into the lives of those who are in desperate need of a Savior.

The house in this verse refers to our lives. If we take time to serve Jesus each day we are slowly building up a beautiful house in His name, but if we only do a little bit here and there we will get comfortable with what we have. Jesus wants so much more for us in our lives! There are so many ways we can serve Him, both big and small. We don't always have to go on a mission trip in order to minister to others; our ministry is right outside our door. We just have to take that first step outside. It is so easy to get caught up in the comfort of our own lives, but we were called to be different. Ephesians 2:8–10 puts it simply, "For it is by grace you have been saved, through faith—and this is not from yourselves, it is the gift of God—not by works, so that no one can boast. For we are God's handiwork, created in Christ Jesus to do good works, which God prepared in advance for us to do."

It is never too late to start building God's Kingdom. Pray for the boldness to step out of your comfort zone. See how you can get involved in your church or in a Bible study, witness to the co-worker or neighbor who has been on your heart, or start out your morning by praying for God to use you in some way that day to build up His house. How wonderful it will be if, on the day we get to meet Jesus, He says to us, "Look at the beautiful house you have made in my Name! All of the intricate detail you put into it. You have served Me well!"

COFFEE CINNAMON ROLL BREAKFAST RING

There is nothing better than a cinnamon roll with a hot cup of coffee in the morning, so combining the two just makes perfect sense.

INGREDIENTS:

1 cup plus 4 tablespoons Sugar

¼ cup Warm Water

1 package Active Dry Yeast

3 cups Unbleached All-Purpose Flour

1 teaspoon Salt

1 cup Unsalted Butter, softened

½ cup Whole Milk

3 large Egg Yolks

1 teaspoon Vanilla

1 cup Salted Butter, melted

Generous sprinkling of Cinnamon

COFFEE FROSTING:

1 box Powdered Sugar (1 pound)

2 teaspoons Maple Flavoring

1 teaspoon Vanilla

¼ cup Milk

3 tablespoons Butter, melted

⅓ cup Brewed Dark Coffee

Dash of Salt

Preheat the oven to 350 degrees.

In a small bowl, without stirring, add 1 tablespoon of sugar, the warm water, and then sprinkle the yeast on top. Cover with a saucer for about 5 minutes. Uncover, stir briefly, and cover it again until you start to see bubbles forming. Set aside.

In a large bowl, stir together the flour, 3 tablespoons sugar, and salt. Add the softened butter and work it into the flour with your hands until it resembles fine crumbs. Make a well in the center.

In a separate small bowl, whisk together the milk, yolks, vanilla, and yeast mixture. Pour it into the center of the well of the flour mixture and start to work it in all together with a spatula until the dough forms.

To assemble the rolls, remove the dough onto a lightly floured surface using unbleached all-purpose flour. Roll the dough out into a large rectangle; the dough should be rolled out to about ¼ inch thick. Pour 1 cup of the melted butter over the surface of the dough. Use your fingers to spread the butter evenly. Sprinkle the remaining 1 cup of sugar evenly on the top and then a generous amount of ground cinnamon.

Roll the rectangle tightly towards you. Use both hands to keep the roll tight. Don't worry if the filling oozes as you work. When you reach the end, pinch the seam together and flip the roll so that the seam is face down.

With a sharp knife, make one-inch slices and start placing the cut rolls in one big circle, slightly overlapping them at the ends in a Bundt pan or pie pan sprayed with cooking spray. You will slice only half the dough, as this recipe makes two rings. At the end, you will have formed a cinnamon roll ring with an empty circle in the middle. Cover with a towel and let rise for about 15 minutes.

Bake for 30 minutes, until golden brown. (If they need more time to cook, cover with foil and bake for about 5 more minutes.) Don't allow the rolls to become overly brown.

While the rolls are baking, make the coffee icing. In a large bowl, whisk together all frosting ingredients until smooth.

Remove pan from the oven and let cool for 5 minutes. Invert onto a large plate and drizzle half the icing over the top while it's still hot. Repeat the process with the other half of the dough. Makes 2 coffee cinnamon roll breakfast rings.

Jesus said to them, "Come and eat breakfast." Yet none of the disciples dared ask Him, "Who are You?"—knowing that it was the Lord. Jesus then came and took the bread and gave it to them, and likewise the fish.

~John 21:12–13

How to Know Jesus

For God so loved the world that He gave His only begotten Son, that whoever believes in Him should not perish but have everlasting life.

~ John 3:16

If you are unsure that you truly know who Jesus Christ is, if you you are unsure if you have received Jesus Christ into your heart and He's living as your personal Savior, or if you want to know who Jesus is, then stop and pray this prayer to Him:

Heavenly Father,

I know that I am a sinner, but I want to spend eternal life with You. I believe in Your Son, Jesus Christ. I believe that He came to earth and died on the cross for my sins, was buried, and on the third day He rose again. Jesus, I need you to save me. Please come into my heart and be my personal Savior. Please forgive me of my sins and help me to center my life on You. Thank you Lord. I love you. Amen.

If you prayed this prayer today, congratulations! You are now a child of God and will spend eternity with Christ! He is in your heart, and your life will forever be changed. I would love to hear about your decision to receive Jesus Christ as your Savior, and I want to help you get started on your journey with Him. Please email us at info@toriwinkelmanbooks.com.